Read with Me

My Favorite Fairytales

Story retold by Janet Brown
Illustrations by Ken Morton

D1511584

Whitecap Books

What do the three bears do while their porridge cools down?

Goldilocks is also walking in the forest. She picks berries and sings to herself. She gathers flowers.

Walking makes her hungry. The warm sun makes her sleepy. She spies a pretty house in the middle of the trees.

"Maybe I can rest there," she thinks. "Maybe they will feed me."

She does not know that this house belongs to the three bears!

Who does the pretty house in the middle of the trees belong to?

Inside, the table is set for three. There are three chairs — one big chair, one medium-sized chair, and one tiny little chair.

On the table there are three bowls of porridge — one big bowl, one medium-sized bowl, and one tiny little bowl.

There are also three spoons, a pitcher of milk, and a jar of honey.

How many places have been set at the table?

Goldilocks climbs into the big chair first. "This chair is too hard!" she says.

She tastes the porridge in the big bowl. "And this porridge is too hot!"

Next she tries the medium-sized chair. "This chair is too soft!" she says.

She tastes the porridge in the medium-sized bowl. "And this porridge is too cold!"

What is wrong with the big chair that Goldilocks climbs into first?

Goldilocks sits down in the tiny little chair. It is very comfortable. She tastes the porridge in the tiny little bowl. It is not too hot and it is not too cold.

"This is just perfect!" says Goldilocks. She eats every last spoonful of porridge.

But Goldilocks is bigger than Baby Bear. After a while the tiny little chair starts to crack, then it breaks into pieces!

Why does Baby Bear's chair break when Goldilocks sits in it?

Goldilocks is tired. She goes upstairs. She finds three beds - a big bed, a medium-sized bed, and a tiny little bed.

She climbs into the big bed. "This bed is too hard!" she says.

She climbs into the medium-sized bed. "This bed is too soft!" she says.

She climbs into the tiny little bed. It is not too hard, and it is not too soft.

"This is just perfect!" says Goldilocks. She falls fast asleep.

Whose bed does Goldilocks fall asleep in?

The bears return from the forest. "What a nice walk that was!" says Papa Bear. "Let's eat!"

Then he looks at the breakfast table.

"Someone's been sitting in my chair!" growls Papa Bear.

"Someone's been sitting in my chair!" frowns Mama Bear.

"Someone's been sitting in my chair!" wails Baby Bear. "And they've smashed it to pieces!"

Why do you think Baby Bear looks so sad in this picture?

They look at the bowls on the table.

"Someone's been eating my porridge!" growls Papa Bear.

"Someone's been eating my porridge!" frowns Mama Bear.

"Someone's been eating my porridge!" wails Baby Bear. "And they've eaten it all up!"

Whose bowl is empty?

The three bears rush upstairs.
"Someone's been sleeping in my bed!" roars Papa Bear. "Someone's been sleeping in my bed!" cries Mama Bear. "Someone's been sleeping in my bed!" yells Baby Bear. "AND SHE'S STILL HERE!"

At that, Goldilocks opens her eyes. She sees three hairy faces looking down at her — a big face, a medium-sized face, and a tiny little face.
"Help!" she cries. She jumps out of bed and runs all the way home.

The bears are surprised. "Was I too loud?" asks Papa Bear. "Was I too fierce?" asks Baby Bear? "I'll make some more porridge," says Mama Bear. "It's way past breakfast time."

Why does Baby Bear think Goldilocks is running away?

There are eight things wrong with the picture below. Can you find them?

Answers:
1) Baby Bear sitting on Papa Bear's chair
2) Heart design on chair instead of diamonds
3) Mama Bear on roller skates
4) Milk pitcher handle missing
5) Left arm of chair pointing upwards
6) Flying spoons
7) Picture hanging upside down
8) One carved chair leg

On a piece of paper, practise writing these words.
Can you find them again in the story?

"This bed is too hard"

jar of honey

bowl of porridge

tiny little chair

pitcher of milk

Three Little Pigs

Story retold by Janet Brown
Illustrations by Ken Morton

Three little pigs are looking for adventure.

They wave good-bye to their friends and go out into the big, wide world.

What do the three little pigs hope to find in the big, wide world?

The first little pig meets a man carrying straw.

"May I have some straw to build a beautiful house?" he asks.

"Certainly, little pig," says the man.

The first little pig builds himself a straw house. Then he sits down for a nap.

What does the first little pig want to do with the straw?

Nearby lives a mean and hungry wolf. The wolf knocks on the door of the straw house.

"Little pig, little pig, let me come in!" he calls.

"Not by the hair of my chinny chin chin will I open the door and let YOU come in!" cries the little pig.

"Then I'll huff and I'll puff and I'll blow your house down!" roars the wolf.

So he huffs and he puffs, and the straw house falls down. The wolf runs inside and gobbles up the first little pig.

How does the wolf make the straw house fall down?

The second little pig meets a man carrying wood.

"May I have some wood to build a big house?" he asks.

"Certainly, little pig," says the man.

The second little pig builds himself a wooden house. Then he sits down for a nap.

What does the second little pig do after he has built his house?

Soon the wolf comes knocking on the door.

"Little pig, little pig, let me come in!" he calls.

"Not by the hair of my chinny chin chin will I open the door and let YOU come in!" cries the little pig.

"Then I'll huff and I'll puff and I'll blow your house down!" roars the wolf.

So he huffs and he puffs, and he HUFFS and he PUFFS, and the wooden house falls down. The wolf runs inside and gobbles up the second little pig.

What does the wolf do when he has blown down the wooden house?

The third little pig meets a man carrying bricks.

"May I please have some bricks to build a strong house?" he asks.

"Certainly, little pig," says the man.

The third little pig builds himself a brick house. He works late into the night.

What kind of house does the third little pig want to build?

Soon the wolf comes knocking on the door.

"Little pig, little pig, let me come in!" he calls.

"Not by the hair of my chinny chin chin will I open the door and let YOU come in!" cries the little pig.

"Then I'll huff and I'll puff and I'll blow your house down!" roars the wolf.

So he huffs and he puffs, and he HUFFS and he PUFFS. Then he huffs and he puffs some more. But the brick house does not fall down!

Why do you think the third little pig's house doesn't fall down?

The next day the wolf returns.

"Little pig!" he says. "Let us go and dig turnips together tomorrow morning!"

The little pig goes to dig turnips that evening. When the wolf arrives the next morning, the field is empty and the little pig is at home eating turnip stew.

The wolf is very angry. But he says, "Little pig, let us go and pick apples together tomorrow morning!"

When the wolf arrives in the morning, the little pig is already up in the tree.

"Here!" yells the little pig, and he throws a juicy apple at the wolf. Then he jumps down, leaps into a barrel, and rolls away down the hill to his brick house.

What does the third little pig throw at the wolf?

The wolf races after the little pig. He leaps up onto the roof of the brick house.

"I'll get you!" he roars, and he climbs down the chimney.

But the little pig puts a pot of water onto the fire. The wolf falls down the chimney and into the pot. The little pig slams the lid on the wolf's head! Nobody ever sees the wolf again.

And the third little pig lives happily ever after in his brick house.

What happens to the wolf when he comes down the chimney?

Look carefully at both pictures.
There are five differences between them.
Can you spot them?

Answers:
1) Door from cottage
2) Mama Pig's handkerchief
3) Bird on gate
4) Third little pig's handkerchief
5) Trees in the distance

On a piece of paper, practise writing these words.
Can you find them again in the story?

bricks

wolf

pot of water

wood

first little pig

Read with Me

Snow White and the Seven Dwarfs

Story retold by Janet Brown
Illustrations by Ken Morton

Snow is falling, and a black raven flies to the palace window. Inside, the Queen sits sewing. She looks up, and the needle pricks her finger.

The Queen thinks, "I wish I could have a little girl with skin as white as the snow, hair as black as the raven, and lips as red as my blood."

Not long afterward, a princess is born. She has snow-white skin, raven-black hair, and blood-red lips. The King and Queen call her Snow White.

What kind of bird flies to the Queen's window?

Snow White is a beautiful and happy child. But, sadly, the Queen dies. The King marries again. Snow White's stepmother is beautiful, but she is vain and cruel. She asks her magic mirror:

"Mirror, mirror on the wall,
Who is the fairest of them all? "

The mirror always replies:

"You, oh Queen, are the fairest of them all."

Who tells the new Queen that she is fairest of them all?

But every year Snow White grows more beautiful. One day the mirror tells the Queen:

"You, oh Queen, are fair, it's true,
But Snow White is more fair than you!"

The Queen is furious. She orders a hunter to take Snow White into the forest and kill her.

But Snow White is kind and pure. The hunter loves her too much to kill her. He tells her to run away. Then he tells the Queen that Snow White is dead.

Why doesn't the hunter kill Snow White?

Snow White is tired and hungry. She is scared and lonely. She wanders into the forest until she sees a house.

Inside, the table is set for dinner. There are seven little chairs and seven little bowls. Snow White takes a little food from each bowl.

Upstairs there are seven little beds. Snow White climbs into one of the beds. She falls fast asleep.

How many people do you think live in the house in the forest?

The house belongs to seven dwarfs. All day long they dig for diamonds in the mountain.

In the evening, when they return home, they see that somebody has taken food from each bowl. They go upstairs, and there in one of the seven little beds is Snow White!

Snow White tells the seven dwarfs about the wicked Queen. They invite her to stay with them. They build her a chair and a bed.

What do the seven dwarfs do on the mountain all day long?

The wicked Queen thinks Snow White is dead. She is as vain as ever. She asks her mirror:

"Mirror, mirror on the wall
Who is the fairest of them all?"

But the mirror replies:

"You, oh Queen, are fair, it's true,
But Snow White is more fair than you!"

The Queen is furious. She decides to kill Snow White herself!

Who does the mirror think is the fairest of them all now?

The Queen dresses as a beggar. When the seven dwarfs have gone to work, the beggar knocks on the door.

"You are such a pretty young thing!" says the beggar to Snow White. "Will you take an apple from a poor, old woman?"

Snow White bites into the rosy, red apple. But the apple is poisoned! Snow White falls down dead. The beggar throws off her disguise.

"Now I am the fairest of them all!" cries the wicked Queen.

Who is the beggar really?

The seven dwarfs weep and wail. They build Snow White a glass coffin, and take her to the top of a hill. They guard her night and day.

One day a prince rides by. He sees Snow White lying there. Her skin is white as snow, her hair is black as a raven, and her lips are red as blood.

"How beautiful she is!" says the prince. He lifts her head to kiss her. The piece of poisoned apple flies out of Snow White's mouth.

Snow White opens her eyes — she is alive! The seven dwarfs dance for joy.

What happens when the prince kisses Snow White?

In the palace, the mirror tells the wicked Queen:

"You, oh Queen, are fair, it's true,
But Snow White is STILL more fair than you!"

The Queen flies into a rage and is never heard of again.

Snow White marries the handsome prince, and they live happily ever after!

Who gets married and lives happily ever after?

On a piece of paper, practise writing these words:

sweeping up

basket

pick axe

shovel

beggar

Look carefully at the seven dwarfs below.

Find three dwarfs with caps pointing to the left.

Which three dwarfs have just one tooth?

Read with Me

The Ugly Duckling

Story retold by Janet Brown
Illustrations by Ken Morton

Mother Duck is very excited. Her eggs are almost ready to hatch. Soon she will be the proud mother of six little ducklings.

Her friend says, "One of your eggs is much bigger than the others."

"ALL my little ducklings will be beautiful," sniffs Mother Duck.

Secretly she is worried. But she does not want the other barnyard animals to know that.

How many little ducklings are about to be born?

It's time! Five eggs start to crack, and five fluffy ducklings wriggle out of their shells.

"Ahhh!" say all the barnyard animals.

Then the sixth egg, the BIG egg, starts to crack. And out steps a very strange bird.

"Oh!" cry the barnyard animals. Then they look at Mother Duck. She pretends not to notice that her sixth baby is a very ugly duckling indeed.

What does Mother Duck pretend not to notice about her sixth duckling?

Mother Duck and her six ducklings go for a swim. Five little ducklings splish splash together in the water. But the sixth duckling is too big to play with the others.

"Ouch!" they cry. "Go away, Ugly Duckling!" They swim away from him, laughing. The Ugly Duckling is unhappy. He decides to run away. But wherever he goes, things are always the same.

"What an ugly duckling!" cry the wild ducks.
"What a strange bird!" cry the geese.
"Go away!" they cry.
"One day," thinks the Ugly Duckling, "I will be beautiful, and then they'll be sorry." But he does not believe it.

What do the Ugly Duckling's brothers and sisters say to him?

The Ugly Duckling is strong and brave. But he is also lonely, and winter is coming. He makes himself a home by the side of a big lake. One morning he wakes up and watches a family of swans flying across the sky.

"How graceful they are!" he thinks. "How happy they must be!"

He sighs. It is getting colder.

Where does the Ugly Duckling make his new home?

Snow begins to fall. The lake freezes over. In the distance the Ugly Duckling can see a farmhouse. There are bright lights and voices.

"I wish I lived over there," he thinks to himself.

But he knows they will only laugh at him.

So he goes out onto the frozen lake instead. His big feet make wonderful skates. The Ugly Duckling skates on the ice for hours. He has fun by himself.

What does the Ugly Duckling do out on the lake by himself?

The ice melts. Spring has come! The other birds start to arrive back at the lake. The water is full of wild ducks and geese, chattering and laughing. They are glad to be together again.

The Ugly Duckling hides. He waits for someone to notice him, but everyone is busy.

Why have the other birds started to arrive back at the lake?

"I don't care," says the Ugly Duckling. He notices everyone else flying around. He stretches his wings and begins to flap. Suddenly he is up in the sky, away from the chattering voices.

"I can fly!" he cries.

The sky is very blue. Up here it is quiet. He feels the sun on his wings. The wind slips past him. It feels wonderful.

Do you recognise the Ugly Duckling in this picture?
Can you guess what has happened?

He flies past a family of swans.

"My goodness!" they say. "What a handsome bird!"

The Ugly Duckling turns around in surprise. "ME?" he asks.

"A most fine and handsome bird!" say the swans. "One of the most beautiful we have ever seen!"

The Ugly Duckling is so surprised that he crashes down into the lake. The he looks into the water to see his reflection.

A snowy white swan is looking back up at him!

What does the Ugly Duckling see reflected in the lake?

All the swans crowd around him. "He must be a prince," they say. "We would like to be his friend."

"Where do you come from?" they ask. "Why haven't we seen you before?"

The Beautiful Swan smiles. "I've been here all the time!" he says.

What is the Ugly Duckling's new name?

On a piece of paper, practise writing these words:

flying south

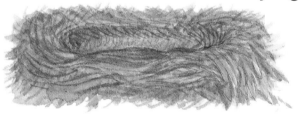

nest

eggs

swan

duckling